D0475411

TEAM SPIRIT ®

SMART BOOKS FOR YOUNG FANS

THE OAKLAND RAIDERS

BY
MARK STEWART

WITHDRAWN

NORWOOD HOUSE PRESS

CHICAGO, ILLINOIS

Norwood House Press
P.O. Box 316598
Chicago, Illinois 60631

For information regarding Norwood House Press, please visit our website at:
www.norwoodhousepress.com or call 866-565-2900.

All photos courtesy of Getty Images except the following:
Icon SMI (4)
Black Book Partners (6, 8, 9, 10, 11, 14, 18, 23, 34 right, 35 top right & bottom, 36, 39, 41, 45),
Pyramid Publications (7), Author's Collection (15, 33),
Topps, Inc. (20, 22, 30, 35 top left, 38, 42 bottom, 43 both), Xerographics, Inc. (21),
Pro/NFL Properties, Inc. (29), Mar-Ja Publications (31), Oakland Raiders/NFL (40),
Cord Communications Corp. (42 top), Matt Richman (48).
Cover Photo: Icon SMI

The memorabilia and artifacts pictured in this book are presented for educational and informational purposes,
and come from the collection of the author.

Editor: Mike Kennedy
Designer: Ron Jaffe
Project Management: Black Book Partners, LLC.
Special thanks to Topps, Inc.

Library of Congress Cataloging-in-Publication Data

Stewart, Mark, 1960-
    The Oakland Raiders / by Mark Stewart. -- Rev. ed.
        p. cm. -- (Team spirit)
    Includes bibliographical references and index.
    Summary: "A revised Team Spirit Football edition featuring the Oakland
Raiders that chronicles the history and accomplishments of the team.
Includes access to the Team Spirit website which provides additional
information and photos"--Provided by publisher.
    ISBN 978-1-59953-534-0 (library edition : alk. paper) -- ISBN
978-1-60357-476-1 (ebook)
    1. Oakland Raiders (Football team)--History--Juvenile literature. I.
Title.
    GV956.O24S74 2012
    796.332'6409794'66--dc23

                                                        2012014901

© 2013 by Norwood House Press.
Team Spirit® is a registered trademark of Norwood House Press.
All rights reserved.
No part of this book may be reproduced without written permission from the publisher.
•••••
The Oakland Raiders is a registered trademark of Oakland Raiders, A California Limited Partnership.
This publication is not affiliated with Oakland Raiders, A California Limited Partnership,
The National Football League, or The National Football League Players Association.

Manufactured in the United States of America in North Mankato, Minnesota.
205N—082012

COVER PHOTO: The Raiders have always had a special bond with their fans.

Table of Contents

ABOUT OUR GLOSSARY

In this book, there may be several words that you are reading for the first time. Some are sports words, some are new vocabulary words, and some are familiar words that are used in an unusual way. All of these words are defined on page 46. Throughout the book, sports words appear in **bold type**. Regular vocabulary words appear in *bold italic type*.

Meet the Raiders

Every sports team plays to win. The Oakland Raiders are no different. What sets them apart from the rest of the **National Football League (NFL)** is that they also play to prove a point. The Raiders and their fans believe that it's good to be different. They like to do things their own way.

Sometimes that is a good plan, and sometimes it is not. When a team experiments with new ideas or gives a chance to *overlooked* players, there is no guarantee of victory. But the fans can expect exciting football week after week. As the Raiders' owner used to tell his players every Sunday, "Just win, baby!"

This book tells the story of the Raiders. There is a family feel in the team's locker room, and the players remain close years after they hang up their uniforms. Whether you take the field for the "silver and black" or root for them, you can count on being a Raider for life.

Michael Huff and Tyvon Branch celebrate a good defensive play.

Glory Days

California and Minnesota are more than 1,500 miles apart. However, the Raiders have always been linked to both states. In 1960, the **American Football League (AFL)** planned to begin its first season with a team in Minnesota. At the last minute, the owners of that club decided they would rather join the NFL. The AFL quickly replaced them with a team in Oakland, California, and called them the Raiders.

The team struggled at first. The Raiders won only nine games in their first three seasons. In 1963, Al Davis was hired to coach the team on the field and run its business off the field. He built the Raiders around talented, young players such as Jim Otto, Clem Daniels, Tom Flores, and Fred Williamson. Oakland had a winning record in its first season under Davis.

The Raiders kept adding good players through smart trades and the **draft**. From

1965 to 1980, Oakland had a winning record every year. During the 1960s, the team's stars included Daryle Lamonica, Fred Biletnikoff, Billy Cannon, Warren Wells, Gene Upshaw, Ben Davidson, Tom Keating, Dan Conners, David Grayson, and Willie Brown.

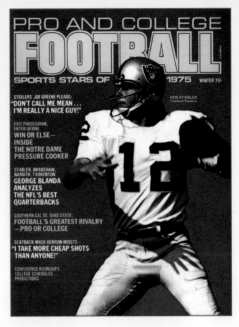

In 1966, the AFL and NFL agreed it would be best to join forces. The merger was set for 1970. A big step in their *strategy* was starting the **Super Bowl**, which matched the winner of each league for the championship of *professional* football. The Raiders won the AFL title in 1967 and played in Super Bowl II. Unfortunately, they lost to the Green Bay Packers.

Oakland's next trip to the Super Bowl came nine years later, under coach John Madden. Quarterback Ken Stabler led the offense. His receivers included Biletnikoff, Dave Casper, and speedy Cliff Branch. Oakland's defense was known as the "Legion of Doom." It starred John Matuszak, Otis Sistrunk, Ted Hendricks, Phil Villapiano, and Jack Tatum. This group led the Raiders to victory in Super Bowl XI.

LEFT: Al Davis watches the clock tick down on another Oakland victory.
ABOVE: Ken Stabler made the Raiders front-page news in the 1970s.

The Raiders won the Super Bowl twice more in the early 1980s. Their coach was Flores, the club's quarterback from the 1960s. Quarterback Jim Plunkett guided the offense. The defense featured Hendricks, Lester Hayes, Rod Martin, Matt Millen, and Howie Long. These teams were rough and tough, and they loved to win.

The Raiders also loved playing for the fans of Oakland. But Davis didn't always get along with city officials. In 1982, the Raiders moved to Los Angeles, in the southern part of California. They played there for 13 seasons. Their stars included Marcus Allen, Todd Christensen, Tim Brown, Bo Jackson, Steve Wisniewski, Vann McElroy, and Terry McDaniel. The team also welcomed players who had been stars with other teams, such as Bob Golic, Jay Schroeder, Jeff Hostetler, Willie Gault, Ronnie Lott, and Mike Haynes.

Allen and Brown were the best of the group. Allen retired as the team's all-time leading rusher. Brown set just about every team receiving record.

LEFT: Marcus Allen barrels through three Washington Redskins to pick up a first down.   **ABOVE**: Tim Brown goes out for a pass.

The Raiders returned to Oakland. They won the **West Division** of the **American Football Conference (AFC)** each season from 2000 to 2002. Quarterback Rich Gannon, kicker Sebastian Janikowski,

and defensive star Charles Woodson led this *era* of success. In January of 2003—after nearly 20 years—the Raiders returned to the Super Bowl. Unfortunately, they lost to the Tampa Bay Buccaneers.

In the years that followed, the Raiders tried to match their success from *decades* past. But the experienced players who led Oakland began to wear down. Brown, Gannon, Jerry Rice, Rod Woodson, and Bill Romanowski either retired or moved on to other teams. The Raiders struggled to rebuild.

Al Davis did what he had always done. He looked for

a mix of young talent and older stars to give the team a winning edge. He wanted rough-and-tumble players who gave their best on every play. Kerry Collins, Warren Sapp, Randy Moss, Ray Buchanan, Richard Seymour, and Carson Palmer all wore the Oakland uniform during this time. The Raiders also drafted Justin Fargas, Michael Huff, Zach Miller, Nnamdi Asomugha, and Darren McFadden.

By 2010, the Raiders were on the rise again. Davis and the fans were feeling their Raider pride. Unfortunately, he passed away during the 2011 season. His son, Mark, took over the team. He shared his father's winning spirit but not his desire to run the team all by himself. The death of the Raiders' longtime leader marked the end of an amazing chapter in football history ... and the start of an exciting new one in Oakland.

LEFT: Rich Gannon   **ABOVE**: Nnamdi Asomugha

Home Turf

The Raiders have hosted their games in three cities. During their first six seasons, they played in the San Francisco area. In 1966, the Raiders moved into a new home, Oakland-Alameda County Stadium. They stayed there until 1982, when they moved again, this time to Los Angeles. The team played there for more than a decade. The Raiders moved back to Oakland for the 1995 season.

The team's stadium in Oakland has changed names many times over the years. The Raiders share it with the Oakland A's baseball team. In 2006, the stadium named the booth where broadcasters announce games after Bill King. He had been the play-by-play voice for the Raiders and A's for more than 40 years.

BY THE NUMBERS

- The Raiders' stadium has 63,026 seats.
- When the stadium expanded in 2006, 10,000 seats were added in a section that was nicknamed "Mount Davis."
- Between original construction and improvements, the stadium cost more than $225 million to build.

Fans pack into the Raiders' stadium for a game.

Dressed for Success

The Raiders have worn their famous silver and black uniforms since 1963. But Oakland's first colors were black and gold. The team used black helmets with a white stripe and no *logo*. Al Davis replaced them with a silver helmet with a black stripe.

Davis also added the team logo to the helmet. It showed a pirate wearing a football helmet, along with a shield and two crossed swords. The logo has become one of the best known in sports.

Today, the Raiders wear uniforms that are almost identical to their style from the 1960s. They usually play in black jerseys for home games. Occasionally, the Raiders wear white at home. They did that for the first time in 2008 to cool down when the temperature on the field soared above 90 degrees.

LEFT: Darren McFadden cools off in the team's white jersey.
RIGHT: Ted Hendricks signed this photo that shows him wearing the famous silver and black.

We Won!

The Raiders rose to the top of professional football in the late 1960s and early 1970s. Oakland won its division seven times in eight seasons. The team captured its first title in 1967 when it took the AFL championship.

Nine years later, the Raiders put it all together and won their first Super Bowl. They went 13–1 in the regular season and then won a thrilling playoff game against the New England Patriots. Trailing in the fourth quarter, Ken Stabler led two late touchdown drives to produce a 24–21 victory. Next, Oakland beat the Pittsburgh Steelers in the AFC title game to earn a trip to Super Bowl XI.

The Raiders went into the Super Bowl feeling that they couldn't lose. The Minnesota Vikings were helpless

LEFT: Pete Banaszak powers through the defense in Super Bowl XI.
RIGHT: Matt Millen celebrates the team's win over the Philadelphia Eagles.

against the powerful Oakland defense. The Raiders led 16–0 after two quarters and continued to roll in the second half. Moments after Pete Banaszak ran for his second touchdown of the game, Willie Brown **intercepted** a pass and went 75 yards for another score. The Raiders won easily, 32–14.

Oakland's next championship came against the Philadelphia Eagles in Super Bowl XV. The Raiders made the playoffs with a team full of *castoffs* from other clubs. Quarterback Jim Plunkett, running back Kenny King, and defensive end John Matuszak were signed by Al Davis after their old teams had given up on them.

Against the Eagles, the Raiders were unstoppable. Plunkett threw two touchdown passes in the first quarter. The first went to Cliff Branch. The second was an 80-yard strike to King. Meanwhile, the Oakland defense was *dominant*. Matt Millen made plays all over

the field, and Rod Martin intercepted three passes. The Raiders cruised to a 27–10 victory.

Three years later, the Raiders—now playing in Los Angeles—faced the Washington Redskins in Super Bowl XVIII. Plunkett was still the quarterback, but new young stars led the team. Marcus Allen ran for more than 1,000 yards and tight end Todd Christensen caught more than 90 passes during the 1983 season. The defense starred Millen, Howie Long, and Lester Hayes.

The Redskins were the defending Super Bowl champions. Earlier in the year, they had defeated the Raiders in an exciting contest, 37–35. In the first half of their rematch, John Riggins could find no running room against the Los Angeles defense. When the Redskins tried to pass, Hayes and Mike Haynes blanketed the Washington receivers.

The Raiders held a 14–3 lead just before halftime. With 12 seconds left, Washington tried a short pass. Linebacker Jack Squirek plucked it out of the air and ran the interception back for a touchdown. Oakland poured it on in the second half. The play that broke the game open was a 74-yard run by Allen. The Raiders won their third NFL championship, 38–9. Allen set a Super Bowl record with 191 rushing yards.

LEFT: Jim Plunkett spots an open receiver.   **ABOVE**: Marcus Allen breaks into the clear on his 74-yard touchdown run in Super Bowl XVIII.

Go-To Guys

To be a true star in the NFL, you need more than fast feet and a big body. You have to be a "go-to guy"—someone the coach wants on the field at the end of a big game. Raiders fans have had a lot to cheer about over the years, including these great stars …

THE PIONEERS

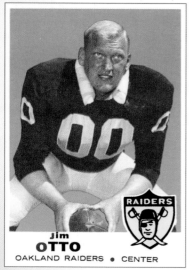

Jim OTTO
OAKLAND RAIDERS • CENTER

JIM OTTO — Offensive Lineman

- BORN: 1/5/1938 • PLAYED FOR TEAM: 1960 TO 1974

Jim Otto did not miss a game during his entire career in Oakland. That was amazing since most teams thought he was too small to play pro football. Otto signed with the Raiders, built up his body, and played center for 15 seasons.

FRED BILETNIKOFF — Receiver

- BORN: 2/23/1943 • PLAYED FOR TEAM: 1965 TO 1978

"Too small, too slow"—that is what the scouts said about Fred Biletnikoff. They left out *too smart*. Biletnikoff caught 40 or more passes 10 years in a row. He finished his career with 589 receptions. Biletnikoff was the last pro to play without shoulder pads.

DAVID GRAYSON — Defensive Back

- BORN: 6/6/1939   • PLAYED FOR TEAM: 1965 TO 1970

The Raiders and Kansas City Chiefs have been *rivals* for 50 years. David Grayson was one of the few players who starred for both teams. He led the league with 10 interceptions in 1968 and was an **All-Pro** three times with Oakland.

GEORGE BLANDA — Kicker/Quarterback

- BORN: 9/17/1927   • PLAYED FOR TEAM: 1967 TO 1975

George Blanda was one of the most reliable players in team history. His *clutch* field goals helped Oakland win many games. In 1970, Blanda passed the Raiders to the AFC title game. He retired with the pro football record of 2,002 points.

ART SHELL — Offensive Lineman

- BORN: 11/26/1946   • PLAYED FOR TEAM: 1968 TO 1982

Art Shell was big, fast, and smart. When the Oakland offense needed to open a hole, it looked to him and teammate Gene Upshaw. Later Shell became the first African-American head coach in the NFL's modern era.

KEN STABLER — Quarterback

- BORN: 12/25/1945   • PLAYED FOR TEAM: 1968 TO 1979

Ken Stabler was an accurate passer who had a knack for wriggling out of tight spots. The "Snake" guided Oakland to its first Super Bowl victory. He was voted the NFL **Most Valuable Player (MVP)** in 1974.

LEFT: Jim Otto   **ABOVE**: David Grayson

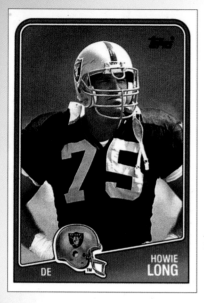

HOWIE LONG — Defensive Lineman

- BORN: 1/6/1960 • PLAYED FOR TEAM: 1981 TO 1993

Teams that played the Raiders in the 1980s usually **double-teamed** Howie Long. Even so, Long was still able to make plays. He had the speed to chase down running backs or **sack** the quarterback.

MARCUS ALLEN — Running Back

- BORN: 3/26/1960 • PLAYED FOR TEAM: 1982 TO 1992

Marcus Allen was a smooth and powerful runner. Each season from 1983 to 1985, he ran for at least 1,000 yards and caught more than 60 passes. Allen was the MVP of Super Bowl XVIII and also the NFL MVP in 1985.

TIM BROWN — Receiver

- BORN: 7/22/1966 • PLAYED FOR TEAM: 1988 TO 2003

Tim Brown spent 16 years catching passes for the Raiders. Brown hauled in more than 1,000 in all. He could do it all, and often did. In 1994, Brown led the AFC in pass receptions and punt returns. By the time he left the game, everyone called him "Mr. Raider."

RICH GANNON — Quarterback

- BORN: 12/20/1965 • PLAYED FOR TEAM: 1999 TO 2004

Rich Gannon struggled through 11 NFL seasons before the Raiders signed him and made him their starting quarterback. Gannon became a great team leader. He was the league MVP in 2002 when he guided Oakland to Super Bowl XXXVII.

CHARLES WOODSON   Defensive Back

- BORN: 10/7/1976
- PLAYED FOR TEAM: 1998 TO 2005

Charles Woodson was a standout from his very first game for the Raiders. In 1998, he was voted Defensive **Rookie** of the Year. Woodson was named to the **Pro Bowl** in each of his first four seasons in Oakland. He had 17 interceptions during his career with the team.

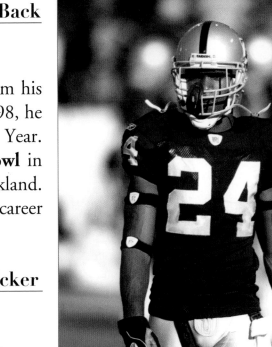

SEBASTIAN JANIKOWSKI   Kicker

- BORN: /2/1978
- FIRST YEAR WITH TEAM: 2000

The Raiders have a proud history of great kickers. Sebastian Janikowski may have been the best of all of them. He had a very strong leg and regularly made **field goals** of more than 50 yards.

SHANE LECHLER   Punter

- BORN: 8/7/1976   • FIRST YEAR WITH TEAM: 2000

Ray Guy was the best punter in team history until Shane Lechler came along. He was voted All-Pro six times in his first 12 seasons. Twice he averaged more than 50 yards per punt, and in 2011 he booted a ball 80 yards.

LEFT: Howie Long   **ABOVE**: Charles Woodson

Calling the Shots

Al Davis was the Oakland coach for just three seasons, but no one had a bigger impact on the team. Davis was successful for many reasons. He created a special togetherness among the players and made them feel like they were part of his family. Davis was also good at finding stars who were overlooked by other teams. In Oakland, they got a warm welcome from teammates and fans.

After he became the team owner, Davis developed a good eye for coaches, too. John Rauch, John Madden, and Tom Flores each led the team to a Super Bowl under him. Rauch was hired to coach the Raiders in 1966, after Davis agreed to become *commissioner* of the AFL. In his second season, Rauch guided Oakland to the league title. But Davis could not resist "helping" Rauch with even the tiniest decisions. So in 1969, Rauch left to coach the Buffalo Bills.

From then on, Davis made it clear to his coaches that they could expect to hear his opinions on a regular basis. That didn't bother Madden. He was promoted to head coach after Rauch left. Madden won 103 games in 10 seasons. Few people loved football the way

John Madden congratulates Cliff Branch after a touchdown.

he did. Under Madden, the Raiders reached the AFC title game five years in a row. They became a truly fearsome team. Madden coached his players to win but also to send a message— no one messes with Oakland!

For Flores, coaching the Raiders was a kind of homecoming. He had been the team's quarterback from 1960 to 1965. Flores was quiet and thoughtful. Sometimes people forgot he was the coach because Davis was in the news so often. But Flores guided the Raiders to victory in the Super Bowl twice—the most of any of the team's coaches.

One Great Day

Teams from California aren't normally used to playing in cold weather, but that's what the Raiders faced against the Browns in Cleveland. In the second round of the playoffs after the 1980 season, the temperature at kickoff was 4 degrees. It was the coldest day for an NFL game since 1967. To make matters worse, the wind was whipping off Lake Erie. The wind made it feel like –37 degrees on the field!

The Browns scored first after intercepting a pass by Jim Plunkett. The Raiders got a boost when they blocked Don Cockroft's extra point. Oakland came back a few minutes later to take the lead. Plunkett handed off to Mark van Eeghen, who barreled into the end zone.

Cleveland bounced back in the third quarter to regain the lead. In the fourth quarter, Oakland put together a long drive. Van Eeghen crossed the goal line again to make the score 14–12. Cleveland fans

Mike Davis intercepts a pass in front of Ozzie Newsome.

were *frustrated*. The Raiders didn't seem to be bothered by the freezing weather at all.

As time was running out, the Browns marched down the field. With the ball on the 13-yard line, Cleveland faced a tough decision. Instead of sending out Cockroft to try the game-winning field goal, the Browns called a pass play. Brian Sipe faded back and saw Ozzie Newsome open in the end zone, but Mike Davis was waiting to swoop in. The Oakland safety made the interception and saved the game. It was a perfect example of why the Raiders were great—they often were at their best when the conditions were at their worst.

Legend Has It

Did a ghost ever play for the Raiders?

LEGEND HAS IT that one did. His name was Dave Casper. He played tight end for Oakland and was named All-Pro four times. Teammates nicknamed him the "Ghost" after the cartoon character Casper the Friendly Ghost. In a 1977 playoff game against the Baltimore Colts, Casper ran a **post pattern** and caught a long pass that helped send the contest into overtime. To this day, Oakland fans call this famous play the "Ghost to the Post."

ABOVE: Dave Casper   **RIGHT**: Jim Plunkett and Tom Flores appear on a magazine cover together. Plunkett, whose family came from Mexico, and Flores both had Latino roots.

Were the Raiders football's greatest pioneers?

LEGEND HAS IT that they were. The Raiders were the first NFL team to hire a Latino coach (Tom Flores) and an African-American coach (Art Shell). They were also the first team to hire a woman to run the

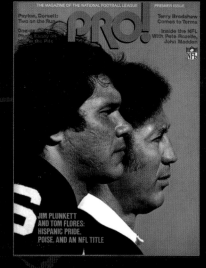

club. Amy Trask began working for the Raiders in college and rose to the position of *Chief Executive Officer (CEO)*.

Who was the NFL's greatest *Star Wars* fan?

LEGEND HAS IT that Lester Hayes was. Hayes was football's top defensive back when he played for the Raiders in the 1970s and 1980s. He wasn't just a *Star Wars* fan—he considered himself a Jedi Knight. Hayes insisted that if Luke Skywalker played football, he would be a cornerback. Teammate Mike Haynes was a believer. At the Pro Bowl one year, Hayes informed Haynes, "The Force has told me that you will wear silver and black next year." He was right. The NFL awarded Haynes to the Raiders in 1983 after a complicated legal battle over his contract.

There isn't much room in pro football for a 40-something quarterback. That's why the Raiders weren't sure what to do with George Blanda in 1970. Blanda had been with the team for three seasons and would soon turn 43. Football was his life. He led the Houston Oilers to the AFL championship in 1960 and 1961. A year later, he was voted league MVP.

Daryle Lamonica

Despite his great career, could Blanda really help the Raiders? It didn't seem like he had much to offer. Besides, Oakland already had two talented passers in Daryle Lamonica and Ken Stabler. But coach John Madden played a hunch and decided that Blanda would serve as the Raiders' kicker and backup quarterback. Sure enough, whenever the Oakland offense struggled, Madden called on the **veteran** to give the team a spark.

LEFT: Daryle Lamonica
RIGHT: This magazine shows George Blanda kicking during the 1970 season. His holder is Lamonica, the player he replaced.

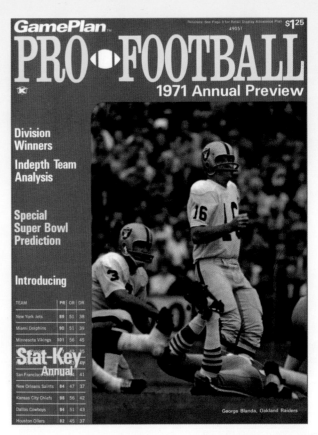

GamePlan™
PRO • FOOTBALL
1971 Annual Preview

Division Winners

Indepth Team Analysis

Special Super Bowl Prediction

Introducing

TEAM	PR	OR	DR
New York Jets	89	51	38
Miami Dolphins	90	51	39
Minnesota Vikings	101	56	45
San Francisco			41
New Orleans Saints	84	47	37
Kansas City Chiefs	98	56	42
Dallas Cowboys	94	51	43
Houston Oilers	82	45	37

Stat-Key Annual

George Blanda, Oakland Raiders

Starting in October, Blanda came off the bench five weeks in a row. He threw three touchdown passes in a win over the Pittsburgh Steelers. He kicked a 48-yard field goal in a last-second tie with the Kansas City Chiefs. A week later, he tossed a scoring pass to tie the Cleveland Browns and then booted the game-winning field goal. Blanda produced victories in the next two weeks, too.

As it turned out, Oakland needed every one of those wins. They edged the Chiefs by one victory to reach the playoffs. Lamar Hunt, the owner of the Chiefs, couldn't believe it. "This George Blanda is as good as his father—who used to play for Houston," Hunt joked at one point.

Blanda got the last laugh. He went on to win the Bert Bell Award as pro football's Player of the Year.

Team Spirit

Oakland fans like to call themselves "Raider Nation." That is because people all over America—and the world—root for the team. In many NFL cities, the Raiders are the second-favorite team.

The fun in Raider Nation starts long before kickoff. Game day in Oakland usually looks like Halloween. The fans wear costumes that are unbelievable! The most famous section of Oakland's stadium is the "Black Hole." Fans there dress all in black and make life for the opposing team miserable.

Some Oakland fans cheer as loud for the Raiderettes as they do for a touchdown. The Raiderettes are the team's silver-and-black dance squad. Competition to be a Raiderette is fierce. Each season the squad holds tryouts—just as the team does for its players.

LEFT: Raiders fans are loud, proud—and different.
ABOVE: Oakland fans wore this patch on their jackets in the 1970s.

Timeline

n this timeline, each Super Bowl is listed under the year it was played. Remember that the Super Bowl is held early in the year and is actually part of the previous season. For example, Super Bowl XLVI was played on February 5, 2012, but it was the championship of the 2011 NFL season.

1963
Clem Daniels leads the AFL in rushing.

1976
The Raiders win their first Super Bowl.

1960
The Raiders play their first AFL season.

1974
Ray Guy is the NFL's top punter.

1980
Lester Hayes is named Defensive Player of the Year.

Ray
Guy

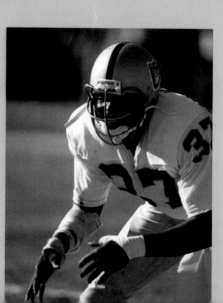

Lester
Hayes

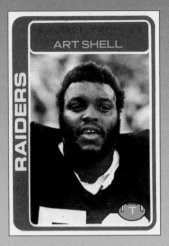

This trading card shows Art Shell during his playing days.

Jerry Rice

1989
Art Shell is named coach of the Raiders.

2002
Jerry Rice makes his 13th Pro Bowl.

2008
Nnamdi Asomugha is named All-Pro.

1984
The Raiders win Super Bowl XVIII.

1997
Tim Brown leads the NFL with 104 receptions.

2011
Shane Lechler makes his sixth Pro Bowl.

Shane Lechler

Fun Facts

KEEP ON RUNNING

After receiver Willie Gault retired from the Raiders in 1993, he went back to his first love, track and field. Gault had been one of the fastest men in the world before his NFL career. In 2011, Gault was crowned the over-50 world champion in the 100 meters.

GOOD NEWS, BAD NEWS

In 2010, the Raiders won every game they played against the teams in their own division. Unfortunately, they fell short of the playoffs. It was the first time in NFL history that this had happened.

CITY BOY

Matt Millen was the first player to win the Super Bowl for four different cities. The All-Pro linebacker won two with the Raiders— one in Los Angeles and one in Oakland—and later captured titles with the San Francisco 49ers and Washington Redskins.

SEA OF HANDS

In 1974, the Miami Dolphins hoped to reach the Super Bowl for a fourth year in a row. The Raiders beat them 28–26 in the playoffs on a touchdown with 24 seconds left in the game. Clarence Davis caught

a desperate pass in the middle of three Miami defenders. The play went down in history as the "Sea of Hands."

HONOR GUARD

After retiring from the Raiders, All-Pro guard Gene Upshaw became the head of the **NFL Players Association**. After he died in 2008, the Raiders added the initials *GU* to their helmets in honor of him.

IT'S A GUY THING

Ray Guy had a leg like a **bazooka**. During the 1976 Pro Bowl, he punted a ball that hit the video screen hanging above the field in the Louisiana Superdome. Guy was voted the NFL's best all-time punter when the league picked its 75th Anniversary team in 1994.

LEFT: Willie Gault   **ABOVE**: Clarence Davis dives to make his game-winning catch against the Miami Dolphins.

Talking Football

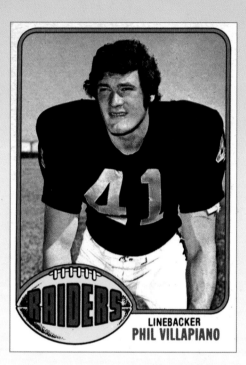

LINEBACKER
PHIL VILLAPIANO

"The players on that 1976 team were very close. If you asked me to pick a guy on that club who 'didn't belong' it would be very difficult."

▶ **Phil Villapiano**, *on the closeness of Oakland's championship team*

"I remember them carrying me off … and I remember them dropping me."

▶ **John Madden**, *on the short victory ride his players gave him after Super Bowl XI*

"We gave 'em something to yell about in the 1970s!"

▶ **Ken Stabler**, *on the exciting Oakland teams of his era*

"He finally found the right fit here."

▶ **Rod Woodson**, *on MVP quarterback Rich Gannon*

"Once a Raider, always a Raider."

▶ *Al Davis*, *on his belief that his players were Raiders for life*

"It has been an honor to wear the Silver and Black."

▶ *Fred Biletnikoff*, *on his career with the Raiders*

"All I ever wanted to do was play. I was never a stat guy."

▶ *Marcus Allen*, *on his love of running with the football*

"George's flair for the **dramatic** highlighted the excitement of pro football during an important period of growth for our sport."

▶ *NFL Commissioner Roger Goodell*, *on George Blanda*

LEFT: Phil Villapiano
ABOVE: Al Davis

Great Debates

People who root for the Raiders love to compare their favorite moments, teams, and players. Some debates have been going on for years! How would you settle these classic football arguments?

The Raiders of the 1970s would beat the Raiders of the 1980s ...

... because they had the perfect balance of offense and defense. The 1976 Raiders outscored their opponents by more than 100 points. They passed for more than 3,000 yards and rushed for more than 2,000 yards. Oakland also made big plays on defense week after week. The Raiders had the NFL's best punter in Ray Guy, too. In Super Bowl XI, Oakland dominated the Minnesota Vikings for their first NFL championship.

Balance? The Raiders of the 1980s were all about balance ...

... because they did not have the great stars that the 1970s teams did. Sure, Marcus Allen and Howie Long made the Pro Bowl, but the players who made the difference were Jim Plunkett, Kenny King ( ), Todd Christensen, Jack Squirek, and Rod Martin. That's what made the Raiders of the 1980s so dangerous. They got the job done with good players having great games.

In 2002, Rich Gannon had the greatest year of any Raiders quarterback ...

... because he led the NFL with more than 400 completions and 4,600 passing yards. He threw 26 touchdown passes and just 10 interceptions. When Gannon (RIGHT) joined the team in 1999, he was considered a **journeyman**. Three seasons later, he was named MVP of the league and led the Raiders to the Super Bowl— at the age of 37!

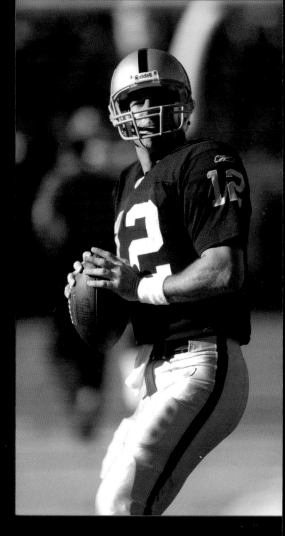

Are you forgetting Ken Stabler? His 1974 season was the greatest ...

... because he narrowly missed leading the Raiders to an undefeated season. Oakland's two losses that year came by one point to the Buffalo Bills and three points to the Denver Broncos. Stabler matched Gannon's 26 scoring passes, but he did it in far fewer attempts. He finished the year as the NFL's highest-rated passer and also was named league MVP.

For the Record

The great Raiders teams and players have left their marks on the record books. These are the "best of the best" …

Daryle Lamonica

Fred Biletnikoff

RAIDERS AWARD WINNERS

WINNER	AWARD	YEAR
Al Davis	AFL Coach of the Year	1963
Archie Matsos	AFL All-Star Game co-MVP	1964
Daryle Lamonica	AFL Most Valuable Player	1967
John Rauch	AFL Coach of the Year	1967
Daryle Lamonica	AFL Most Valuable Player	1969
Ken Stabler	NFL Offensive Player of the Year	1974
Ken Stabler	NFL Most Valuable Player	1974
Fred Biletnikoff	Super Bowl XI MVP	1976
Jim Plunkett	NFL Comeback Player of the Year	1980
Jim Plunkett	Super Bowl XV MVP	1980
Lester Hayes	NFL Defensive Player of the Year	1980
Lyle Alzado	NFL Comeback Player of the Year	1982
Marcus Allen	NFL Offensive Rookie of the Year	1982
Marcus Allen	Super Bowl XVIII MVP	1983
Marcus Allen	NFL Most Valuable Player	1985
Charles Woodson	NFL Defensive Rookie of the Year	1998
Rich Gannon	Pro Bowl MVP	2001
Rich Gannon	Pro Bowl MVP	2002
Rich Gannon	NFL Most Valuable Player	2002

RAIDERS ACHIEVEMENTS

ACHIEVEMENT	YEAR
AFL West Champions	1967
AFL Champions	1967
AFL West Champions	1968
AFL West Champions	1969
AFC West Champions	1970
AFC West Champions	1972
AFC West Champions	1973
AFC West Champions	1974
AFC West Champions	1975
AFC West Champions	1976
AFC Champions	1976
Super Bowl XI Champions	1976*
AFC Champions	1980
Super Bowl XV Champions	1980*
AFC West Champions	1982
AFC West Champions	1983
AFC Champions	1983
Super Bowl XVIII Champions	1983*
AFC West Champions	1985
AFC West Champions	1990
AFC West Champions	2000
AFC West Champions	2001
AFC West Champions	2002
AFC Champions	2002

Super Bowls are played early the following year, but the game is counted as the championship of this season.

Billy
CANNON
OAKLAND RAIDERS • END

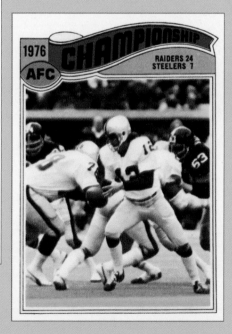

TOP: Billy Cannon was a star for the 1967 AFL champs.
RIGHT: This trading card celebrates Oakland's 1976 AFC title.

43

Pinpoints

The history of a football team is made up of many smaller stories. These stories take place all over the map—not just in the city a team calls "home." Match the pushpins on these maps to the **Team Facts**, and you will begin to see the story of the Raiders unfold!

TEAM FACTS

1 Oakland, California—*The Raiders played here starting in 1960.*

2 Los Angeles, California—*The Raiders played here from 1982 to 1994.*

3 Dallas, Texas—*Tim Brown was born here.*

4 Yazoo City, Mississippi—*Willie Brown was born here.*

5 Foley, Alabama—*Ken Stabler was born here.*

6 Swainsboro, Georgia—*Ray Guy was born here.*

7 Wausau, Wisconsin—*Jim Otto was born here.*

8 Welch, West Virginia—*Rod Martin was born here.*

9 North Little Rock, Arkansas—*Darren McFadden was born here.*

10 Erie, Pennsylvania—*Fred Biletnikoff was born here.*

11 Walbrzych, Poland—*Sebastian Janikowski was born here.*

12 Guatemala City, Guatemala—*Ted Hendricks was born here.*

Darren McFadden

45

Glossary

ALL-PRO—An honor given to the best players at their positions at the end of each season.

AMERICAN FOOTBALL CONFERENCE (AFC)—One of two groups of teams that make up the NFL.

AMERICAN FOOTBALL LEAGUE (AFL)—The football league that began play in 1960 and later merged with the NFL.

BAZOOKA—A weapon that can launch rockets.

CASTOFFS—Unwanted people who are set adrift.

CHIEF EXECUTIVE OFFICER (CEO)—The person who makes all the important decisions for a team or company.

CLUTCH—Good under pressure.

COMMISSIONER—The person in charge of a professional league.

DECADES—Periods of 10 years; also specific periods, such as the 1950s.

DOMINANT—Ruling or controlling.

DOUBLE-TEAMED—Blocked with two players.

DRAFT—The annual meeting during which teams choose from a group of the best college players.

DRAMATIC—Something that is sudden or surprising.

ERA—A period of time in history.

FIELD GOALS—Goals from the field, kicked over the crossbar and between the goal posts. A field goal is worth three points.

FRUSTRATED—Disappointed and puzzled.

INTERCEPTED—Caught in the air by a defensive player.

JOURNEYMAN—A player who has been on many teams without a lot of success.

LOGO—A symbol or design that represents a company or team.

MOST VALUABLE PLAYER (MVP)—The award given each year to the league's best player; also given to the best player in the Super Bowl and Pro Bowl.

NATIONAL FOOTBALL LEAGUE (NFL)—The league that started in 1920 and is still operating today.

NFL PLAYERS ASSOCIATION—The organization that represents the NFL players in all business matters.

OVERLOOKED—Ignored or not noticed.

POST PATTERN—A pass play in which a receiver runs toward the goal posts.

PRO BOWL—The NFL's all-star game, played after the regular season.

PROFESSIONAL—Paid to play.

RIVALS—Extremely emotional competitors.

ROOKIE—A player in his first season.

SACK—Tackle the quarterback behind the line of scrimmage.

STRATEGY—A plan or method for succeeding.

SUPER BOWL—The championship of the NFL, played between the winners of the National Football Conference and American Football Conference.

VETERAN—A player with great experience.

WEST DIVISION—A group of teams that play in the western part of the country.

OVERTIME

TEAM SPIRIT introduces a great way to stay up to date with your team! Visit our **OVERTIME** link and get connected to the latest and greatest updates. **OVERTIME** serves as a young reader's ticket to an exclusive web page—with more stories, fun facts, team records, and photos of the Raiders. Content is updated during and after each season. The **OVERTIME** feature also enables readers to send comments and letters to the author! Log onto:

www.norwoodhousepress.com/library.aspx

and click on the tab: **TEAM SPIRIT** to access **OVERTIME**.

Read all the books in the series to learn more about professional sports. For a complete listing of the baseball, basketball, football, and hockey teams in the **TEAM SPIRIT** series, visit our website at:

www.norwoodhousepress.com/library.aspx

On the Road

OAKLAND RAIDERS
7000 Coliseum Way
Oakland, California 94621
510-864-5000
www.raiders.com

THE PRO FOOTBALL HALL OF FAME
2121 George Halas Drive NW
Canton, Ohio 44708
330-456-8207
www.profootballhof.com

On the Bookshelf

To learn more about the sport of football, look for these books at your library or bookstore:

- Frederick, Shane. *The Best of Everything Football Book.* North Mankato, Minnesota: Capstone Press, 2011.

- Jacobs, Greg. *The Everything Kids' Football Book: The All-Time Greats, Legendary Teams, Today's Superstars—And Tips on Playing Like a Pro.* Avon, Massachusetts: Adams Media Corporation, 2010.

- Editors of *Sports Illustrated for Kids. 1st and 10: Top 10 Lists of Everything in Football.* New York, New York: Sports Illustrated Books, 2011.

Index

About the Author

MARK STEWART has written more than 50 books on football and over 150 sports books for kids. He grew up in New York City during the 1960s rooting for the Giants and Jets, and was lucky enough to meet players from both teams. Mark comes from a family of writers. His grandfather was Sunday Editor of *The New York Times,* and his mother was Articles Editor of *Ladies' Home Journal* and *McCall's.* Mark has profiled hundreds of athletes over the past 25 years. He has also written several books about his native New York and New Jersey, his home today. Mark is a graduate of Duke University, with a degree in history. He lives and works in a home overlooking Sandy Hook, New Jersey. You can contact Mark through the Norwood House Press website.

31901051652859